WHEN A KID LIKE ME FIGHTS CANCER

illustrated by
Angel Chang

Catherine Stier

Albert Whitman & Company
Chicago, Illinois

For all the young fighters—CS

To all the brave in the world—AC

The National Pediatric Cancer Foundation is dedicated to funding research to eliminate childhood cancer. Our focus is to find less toxic, more targeted therapies through a unique collaborative research initiative called the Sunshine Project. NPCF's innovative research consortium brings together the nation's top pediatric oncology specialists to fast-track new treatments and increase the survival rate for children battling cancer.

Library of Congress Cataloging-in-Publication data is on file with the publisher.

Text copyright © 2019 Catherine Stier
Illustrations copyright © 2019 by Albert Whitman & Company
Illustrations by Angel Chang
Hardcover edition first published in the United States of American in 2019 by Albert Whitman & Company
Paperback edition first published in the United States of America in 2021 by Albert Whitman & Company
ISBN 978-O-8075-6396-O (paperback)
ISBN 978-O-8075-6392-2 (ebook)

Printed in China
10 9 8 7 6 5 4 3 2 1 RRD 24 23 22 21 20

Design by Ellen Kokontis

For more information about Albert Whitman & Company,
visit our website at www.albertwhitman.com.

INTRODUCTION

Twenty-seven years ago, I faced a terrifying reality; my infant daughter had cancer.

While still dealing with the shock of diagnosis, I was surprised to learn that there was very little funding for research for pediatric cancers. Many of the protocols and drugs were passed down from the adult world of oncology and had seen no improvement in many years.

Like many, I felt this was unacceptable. Along with another parent, I began to raise money to fund pediatric cancer research in order to improve treatment for all children dealing with cancer with the dream of one day eradicating cancer from children. This was the basis on which the National Pediatric Cancer Foundation was formed.

Today the National Pediatric Cancer Foundation is leading research efforts to save and improve the lives of children suffering from cancer. NPCF's unique collaborative model funds hope through a fast, nimble approach to research in order to find a cure faster.

In addition to research, NPCF also funds a Safety Net program and an Education program. The Safety Net program offsets patient costs associated with research trial enrollment. The Education program raises community awareness about the challenges and realities of pediatric cancer. *When a Kid Like Me Fights Cancer* is a direct outgrowth of our educational efforts.

I hope this book reaches families that are newly diagnosed and helps them feel less scared and less alone knowing they have a community of support and many others have fought this battle and won.

My dream is that we find new treatments to improve the outcomes for children and young adults facing this disease and, ideally, find a cure.

With hope,

Melissa Helms
Co-Founder & Board Emeritus
National Pediatric Cancer Foundation

We get the news...
    I find out I'm a kid who
has to deal with cancer.
    Cancer.
    I am just learning what
that means.

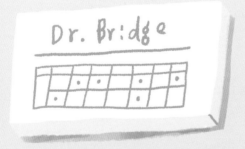

Things move pretty fast, then. And I learn a lot.
My parents and I meet with doctors to decide on a treatment plan. That's a plan for all the things my doctors and my family and I will do to help me beat cancer.
So I learn, first of all, that cancer is something you fight.

I learn other things too. I learn that this cancer is not my fault. It's no one's fault. I didn't catch it from anyone, and no one can get cancer from me. It's just that sometimes, something goes wrong inside the body. Then a good kid has to deal with a bad disease.

ANATOMY

THE HUMAN BODY

My mom calls my teacher, Ms. Stella, to explain why I won't be at school for a while. I get on the phone too.

"We are all rooting for you," Ms. Stella tells me.

I learn that it feels good to have people cheering you on in your fight.

The next afternoon, I tell some of my friends.

"Whoa," says Ramiro. "Cancer. That's serious, right?"

"I didn't know kids got cancer," says Lily.

My best friend, Jeffrey, doesn't say anything at all.

I learn that when you talk about cancer, people don't always know what to say.

Then Jeffrey puts his hand on my shoulder. I learn that people don't always have to speak to show they care about you.

My parents and I visit the hospital so I can tour the places where some of my cancer treatments will happen. At the hospital, I see kids who have already started their treatments. I learn that our stories are all different.

One kid is wearing a superhero cape and painting a picture. Another kid dances by in giant moose slippers. I learn that surprising and even silly things can happen at a hospital.

A hospital volunteer gives me a teddy bear. She tells me that a teenager made it in a high school club. She says that the teenager hopes the teddy bear will make a kid like me smile.

I think maybe I am too old for a teddy bear. And the bear's bow tie—it's ridiculous.

Still, I decide I like this bear anyway. I call him Bowie.

As time goes on, I learn more about what it means to be a kid who is fighting cancer.

I learn that some things do change...

I begin to lose my hair (I wear my baseball cap a lot).

I am tired more often.

I can't always hang out with my friends.

I spend more time inside doing quiet things.

But I also learn that some things don't change...
I can still do lots of my favorite things.
I can still be silly sometimes.
I still laugh with the people who love me.
Sometimes we laugh so hard, we cry.

And sometimes, for other reasons, we just cry.
That's okay too.

I learn from my doctors that medical workers, scientists, and students all over the world are studying, researching, and experimenting to find ways to beat cancer in kids.

And there are people of all ages, like the teenager who made Bowie, who want to help kids like me to be healthier and happier. They want to help however they can.

One day my mom tells me I am an inspiration.
She says lots of folks think I am brave and a hero.
  "Why?" I ask.
  "You show up, you courageous kid, and do what
has to be done. Even grown-ups admire that."

Mom tells me that people in our town are planning a picnic to raise money for childhood cancer research. Everyone at the picnic will wear a gold "Fight Childhood Cancer" ribbon. And they will each wear a big button with my picture on it.

"Really?" I ask. "A picture of me?"

"Let's give them a good one," she says. I grab Bowie and smile my widest smile, and Mom snaps a photo.

I can't be at the picnic that day. But because I sent those picnic people a photo, they send one back to me.

In the photo, there's a group of my neighbors, classmates, and even people I don't know. They wear gold ribbons and buttons with my picture. They each hold up a fierce, fighting fist.

I am a kid who is fighting cancer.
"But you know, Bowie," I say. "I have learned this..."

"I am not fighting alone."